A Colonial Williamsburg
ACTIVITIES BOOK

FUN ACTIVITIES FOR YOUNG VISITORS

Activities by Pat Fortunato
Illustrations by John Wallner

The Colonial Williamsburg Foundation
Williamsburg, Virginia

©1982 The Colonial Williamsburg Foundation   Tenth printing, 2001 Printed in the United States of America   All rights reserved   ISBN: 0-87935-062-8

The Colorful World of Williamsburg

You see colors everywhere in Williamsburg—on the houses and signs, the people's clothes, and the flowers and trees. But this picture needs your help. Color it in to make the scene come to life.

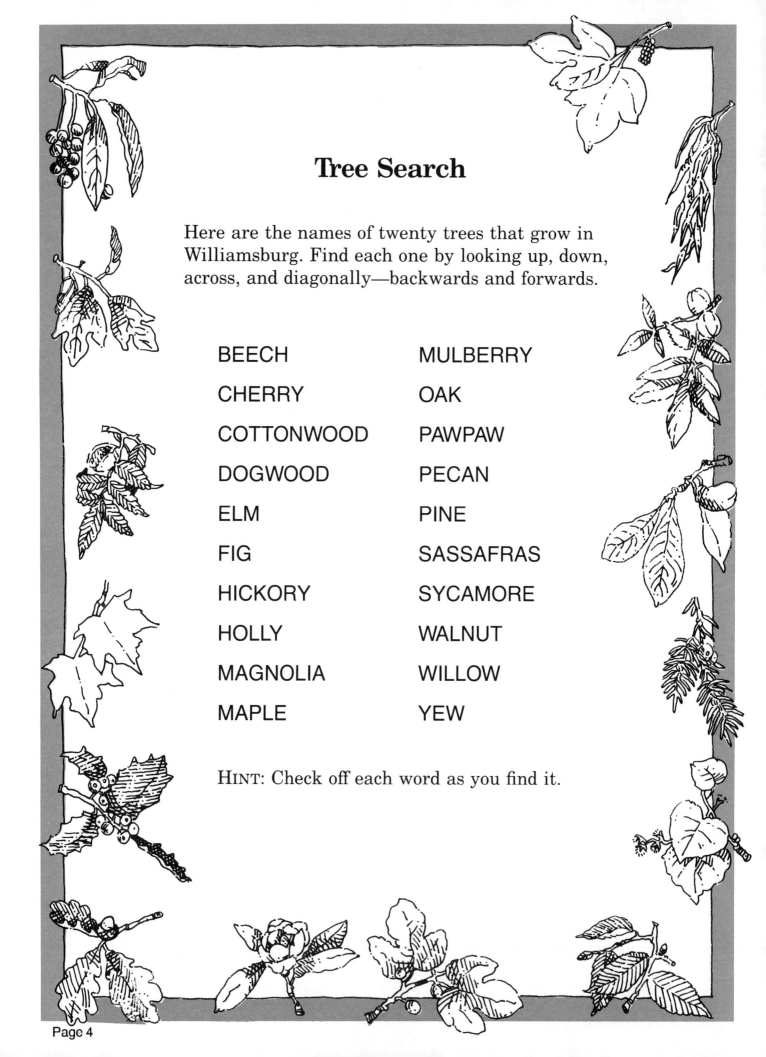

Tree Search

Here are the names of twenty trees that grow in Williamsburg. Find each one by looking up, down, across, and diagonally—backwards and forwards.

BEECH	MULBERRY
CHERRY	OAK
COTTONWOOD	PAWPAW
DOGWOOD	PECAN
ELM	PINE
FIG	SASSAFRAS
HICKORY	SYCAMORE
HOLLY	WALNUT
MAGNOLIA	WILLOW
MAPLE	YEW

HINT: Check off each word as you find it.

C	O	T	T	O	N	W	O	O	D	E
H	M	K	Z	Q	E	N	I	P	E	L
E	J	A	U	M	A	P	L	E	R	M
R	D	O	G	W	O	O	D	C	O	U
R	W	A	L	N	U	T	X	A	M	L
Y	D	Y	L	L	O	H	P	N	A	B
P	A	W	P	A	W	L	B	G	C	E
F	E	B	W	O	L	L	I	W	Y	R
Y	S	A	S	S	A	F	R	A	S	R
B	E	E	C	H	I	C	K	O	R	Y

Building Blocks

Here are some things used to build houses in colonial Williamsburg:

CBKRI, OESNT, IENP, SAGSL, ATPNI

WHAT? YOU DON'T KNOW WHAT ANY OF THEM ARE?
Yes, you do—if you UNSCRAMBLE EACH WORD.

C B K R I = ☐ ☐ ☐ ☐ ☐

O E S N T = ☐ ☐ ☐ ☐ ☐

I E N P = ☐ ☐ ☐ ☐

S A G S L = ☐ ☐ ☐ ☐ ☐

A T P N I = ☐ ☐ ☐ ☐ ☐

This is the house that <u>you</u> built!

Well, maybe not the whole house. All you do is add these finishing touches:

- One door in the center of the front wall.
- Two windows, one on either side of the door. (Give the windows shutters and panes.)
- Four more windows on the second floor, two on either side of the window that's there. (Make all of the windows look the same as the one in the middle.)
- The top of the chimney on the right side of the house.

Try to make all the things you draw look like the things you see in Colonial Williamsburg.

People at Work

On this page, you'll find a basketmaker, a wigmaker, a printer, a cooper (barrel maker), a musical instrument maker, a gunsmith, and a shoemaker.

Write the name of each person's job under the picture. Then draw a line from the person to the thing the person makes. We did one for you to show you how.

COOPER

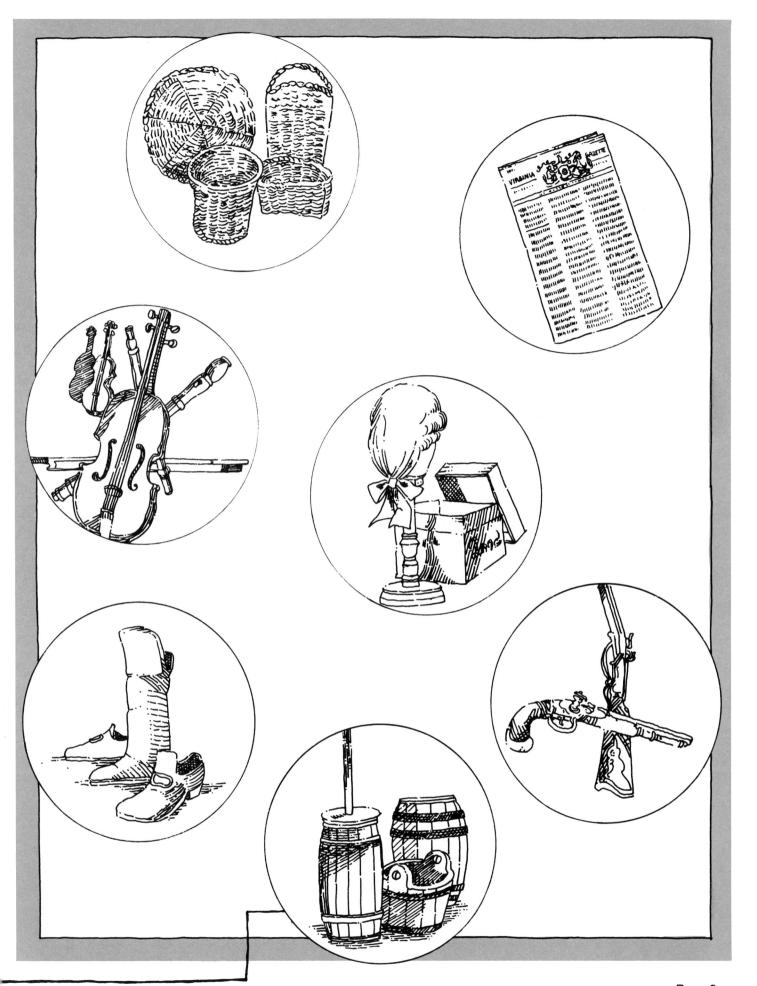

Windmill Crossword

ACROSS

1. Turn, as the windmill's arms do.
4. Opposite of "Slow."
8. "Ready, ____, fire!"
10. The Revolutionary ____.
11. Grain goes ____, flour comes OUT.
12. Goes with "Vigor," rhymes with "Him."
14. You and I.
15. "Magic" sticks.
17. Sound before "Choo!"
18. Landowners brought grain ____ the miller.
20. Robert E. ____ (famous Virginia family).
21. To plant seeds.
22. Louisiana (abbreviation).
24. The wind direction, northeast (abbreviation).
26. "Your," as a colonial Quaker said it.
30. The windmill sits ____ top of a post.
32. From the past.
33. Sounds like "Sow."
34. Colonial hair piece.
36. Opposite of "Him."
37. Opposite of "Fast."
38. Green vegetable eaten in colonial Virginia.

DOWN

1. The part of the windmill that catches the wind.
2. Needle's relative.
3. I am.
5. Sound of disappointment.
6. To cut lumber.
7. What lumber comes from.
9. Air movement.
12. Virginia (abbreviation).
13. Maryland (abbreviation).
15. Grain used for bread.
16. Mill____ (flat round rock for grinding grain).
17. Every one.
19. Have a debt.
23. Place to turn grain into flour.
25. Dairy animals found in colonial Virginia.
27. Laugh sound.
28. North Dakota (abbreviation).
29. Yellow vegetable grown in colonial Virginia.
31. Nothing at all.
33. Sounds like "See."
35. Opposite of "Stop."
36. Opposite of "She."

SPECIAL WORD LIST
Everything you need to fill in the squares is right here:

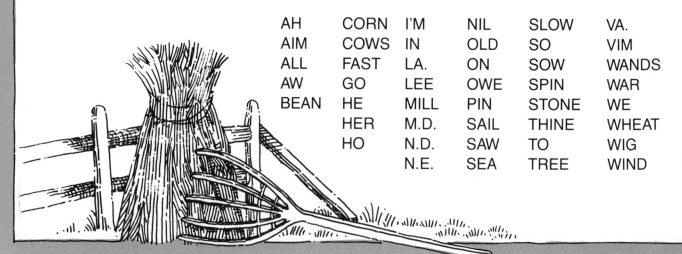

AH	CORN	I'M	NIL	SLOW	VA.
AIM	COWS	IN	OLD	SO	VIM
ALL	FAST	LA.	ON	SOW	WANDS
AW	GO	LEE	OWE	SPIN	WAR
BEAN	HE	MILL	PIN	STONE	WE
	HER	M.D.	SAIL	THINE	WHEAT
	HO	N.D.	SAW	TO	WIG
		N.E.	SEA	TREE	WIND

Go to Your Room!

If you had been a colonial child, you might have had a room like this—and you might have played with SOME of the toys there.

Put an ⊠ in the YES BOX for the toys that are from colonial times. Put an ⊠ in the NO BOX for those that are not.

YES ☐ NO ☐ 1. TEA SET
YES ☐ NO ☐ 2. SKATEBOARD
YES ☐ NO ☐ 3. TOP
YES ☐ NO ☐ 4. PLAYING CARDS
YES ☐ NO ☐ 5. BILBO-CATCHER
YES ☐ NO ☐ 6. TOY WINDMILL

YES ☐ NO ☐ 7. TOY TRUCK
YES ☐ NO ☐ 8. DOLL
YES ☐ NO ☐ 9. PULL TOY
                HORSE
YES ☐ NO ☐ 10. BIRD WHISTLE
YES ☐ NO ☐ 11. TOY PLANE

Which of these toys do YOU play with? Write their names here:

_____

_____

1. _____

2. _____

3. _____

4. _____

Name the Game

Besides the toys on pages 12 and 13, colonial children played many games. You know some of them—hopscotch, leapfrog, blindman's buff, hide and seek. But some are so old that they may be new to you.

Here are the names of five games, and a little bit about how to play them. Try to figure out which name goes with which game. Write each name on the line.

STOOL BALL

A game played with a ball and a stool. The tosser threw the ball and tried to hit the stool. The batter tried to hit the ball away with his hand before it hit the stool.

QUOITS

This game was like pitching horseshoes. Players threw a metal ring toward a *hob* (iron pin). The person—or team—who got nearest to the hob was the winner.

CRICKET

The way it was played in Williamsburg, the bowler threw a ball underhand toward the *wicket,* two foot-high poles with a stick across the top. The striker stood in front of the wicket, defending it, and tried to hit the ball into the field to score runs.

SHUTTLECOCK

This game is like badminton and is played with a racquet called the battledore.

FIVES

This game was like handball. Was it called "Fives" because there were five players? Or because there are five fingers on a hand? Nobody knows for sure.

5.

Picture This

This picture doesn't look like anyone you'd find in Colonial Williamsburg, does it? This picture doesn't look like ANY-ONE, period. That's because it's all mixed up.

To make the picture make sense, copy what you see in each square onto the squares on the next page. *Just be sure to match the numbers.*

1

2

3

4

5

6

7

8

9

10

11

12

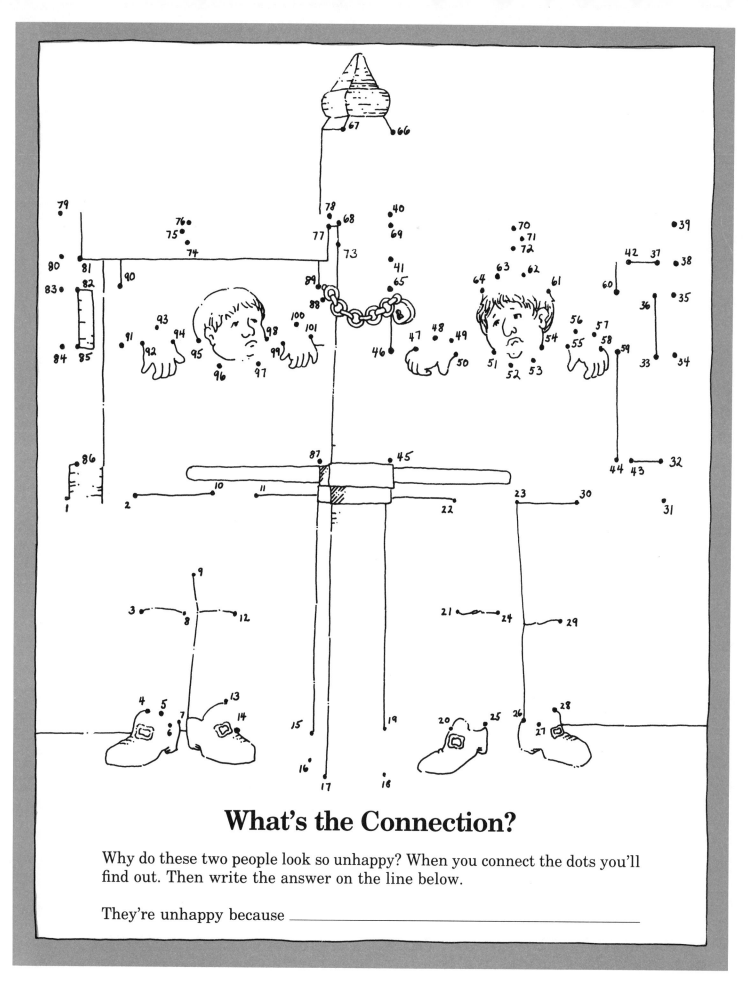

What's the Connection?

Why do these two people look so unhappy? When you connect the dots you'll find out. Then write the answer on the line below.

They're unhappy because _____

The Gaol Game

Starting with GAOL, the colonial way to spell JAIL, fit all the words on this list in the boxes:

3 Letters	4 Letters	5 Letters	6 Letters	7 Letters	8 Letters	9 Letters
BAR	GAOL	CELLS	DEBTOR	PILLORY	PRISONER	HANDCUFFS
	KEYS	CHAIN	KEEPER		SENTENCE	
	LOCK	COURT	STOCKS			
		GUARD	WARDER			
		STEAL				

HINT: There's only one place for words of 3 letters, 7 letters, or 9 letters!

What's Cooking?

Here we are in a colonial kitchen. But wait! Something is wrong. In fact, many things are wrong. We counted 14 things that don't belong in the picture. Find and circle them.

SUDSIO DETERGENT

HURRY-UP GINGERBREAD

(A Slightly Mixed-up Recipe)

INGREDIENTS:

½ cup sugar

½ cup butter

1 egg

1 cup molasses

2 cups flour

1 tablespoon ginger

1 teaspoon cinnamon

½ teaspoon salt

1 cup sour milk*

1 teaspoon baking soda

*To make sour milk: Put a tablespoon of lemon juice or white vinegar in an 8-ounce measuring cup. Fill the cup with milk (at room temperature). Stir and let stand for 10 minutes.

INSTRUCTIONS:

Hurry up and unscramble the key OWDSR = WORDS
Then you can follow the recipe and make the gingerbread.

ABTE = ☐☐☐☐ together the sugar, butter, and egg.

XMI = ☐☐☐ in the molasses.

FTSI = ☐☐☐☐ together the flour, ginger, cinnamon, and salt.

DAD = ☐☐☐ the baking soda to the milk.

Then, take turns adding some
of the flour mixture and some of the
milk mixture to the sugar mixture.

ITSR = ☐☐☐☐ it all up till it's mixed well.

OPUR = ☐☐☐☐ it into a greased pan about 13″ × 9″.

ABEK = ☐☐☐☐ in a 350° oven for about 30 minutes.

IT'S REALLY ODGO = ☐☐☐☐ !

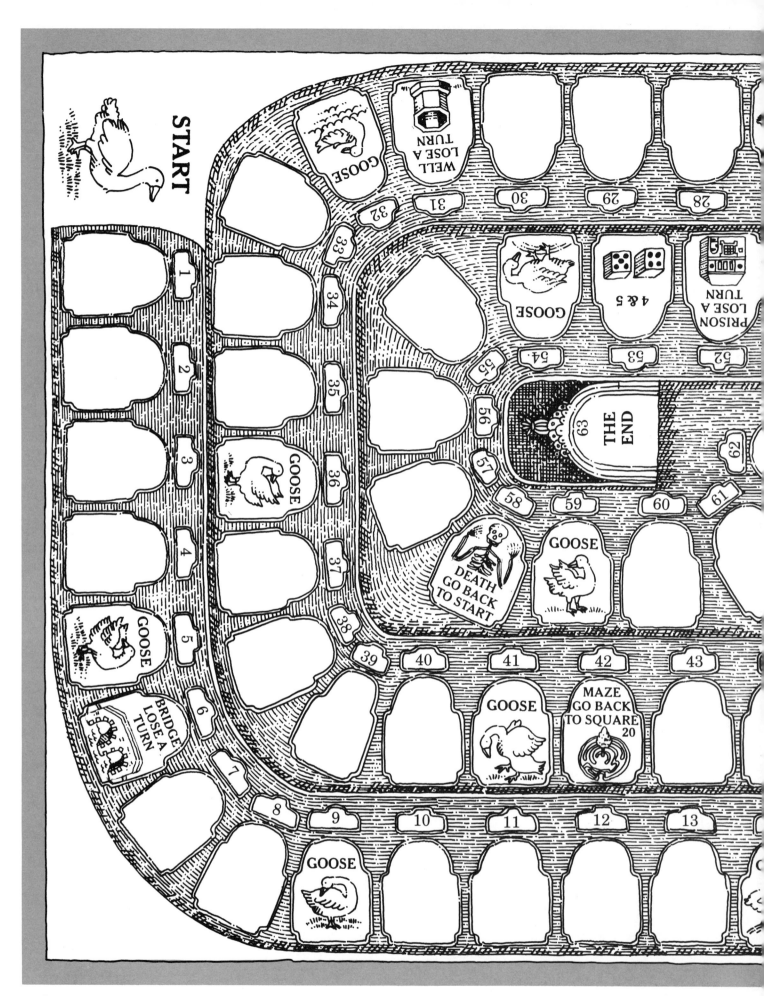

START

THE END

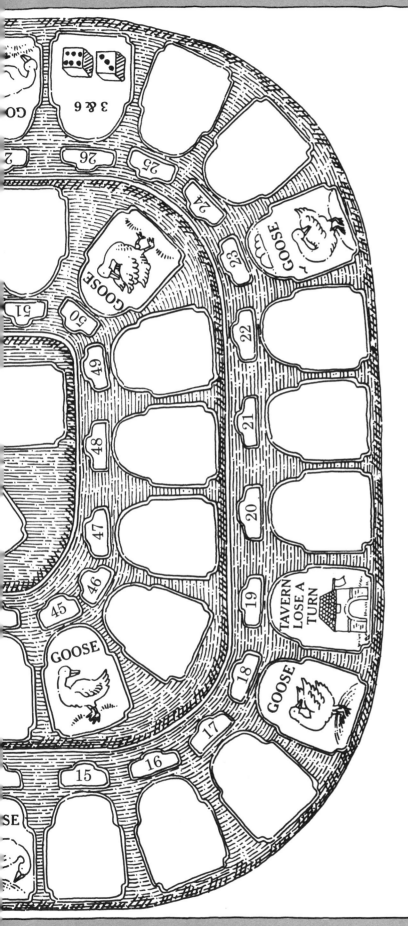

The Game of the Goose

In colonial Williamsburg, people played THE GAME OF THE GOOSE. Even today, adults play the game at night in Chowning's Tavern. We made up a *special* GAME OF THE GOOSE for young people—so you can play it right now, anywhere you are.

This is a race game. You begin on the square marked START, and the first player to reach THE END wins.

HOW TO GET READY:
- Find buttons or coins to use as markers.
- Find a pair of dice, or make number squares by cutting out 12 little pieces of paper. Write the number 1 on two of them, 2 on two more, and so on, right up to number 6. Then take these pieces of paper and put them in a cup or hat.

HOW TO PLAY:
1. Each player rolls the dice or picks out two number squares, adds up the numbers, and moves that many squares on the game board.
2. Some of the squares on the board are special. If you land on them, you have to do whatever they say.
3. If you get a 6 and a 3 on the first try, go to SQUARE 26. If on the next turn you get a 5 and a 4, go to SQUARE 53.
4. When you land on a square with a GOOSE, you have to move forward the same number of squares you just moved until you land on a square without a GOOSE.
5. If you land on SQUARE 58, DEATH, go back to the beginning!

There are many things in the blacksmith's shop. But there are also many words in the word

BLACKSMITH!

RULES: Use each letter only once in a single word. No foreign words, abbreviations, proper names, or brand names. Using a dictionary is okay!

Make as many words as you can from the letters in B L A C K - S M I T H and write them here:

Letter Game

Dear Visitor to Colonial Williamsburg,

Did you go to the Post Office? Then you saw the postmistress seal and stamp the letters.

HERE'S A GAME YOU PLAY WITH LETTERS. Not the kind you mail, but the kind that make up words.

Turn SEND into MAIL by changing only *one letter at a time*. (Use the clues to help.)

Your friends at
Colonial Williamsburg

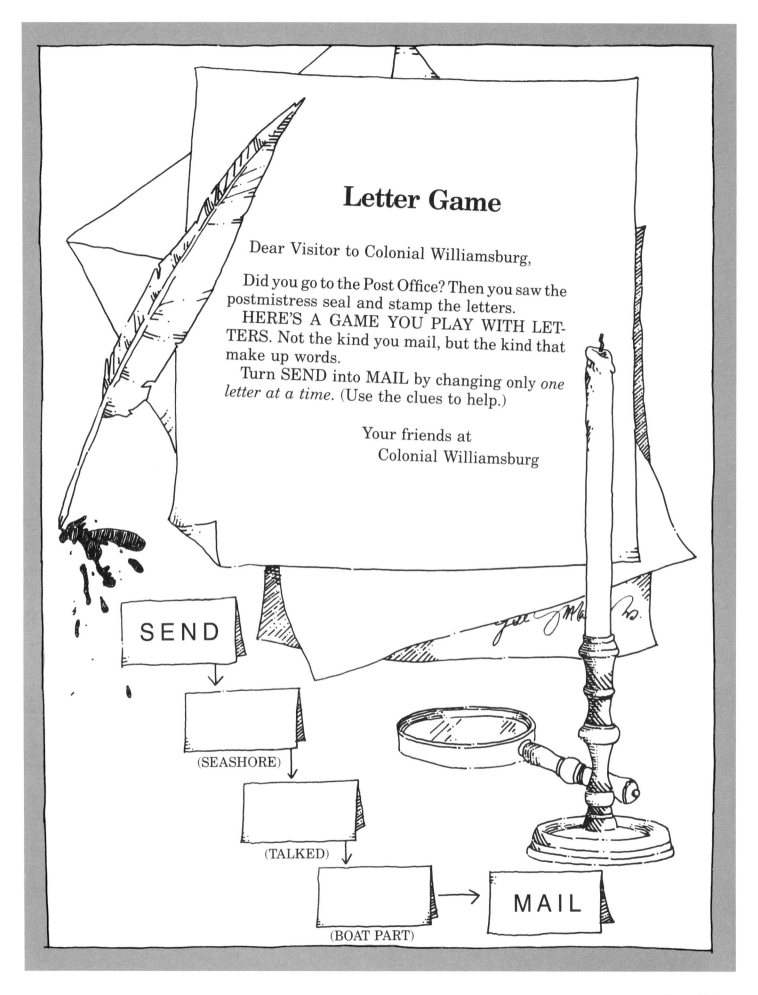

SEND

(SEASHORE)

(TALKED)

(BOAT PART)

MAIL

Alphabet Inkwell

Children who went to school in colonial Williamsburg used quill pens and inkwells. But this inkwell doesn't hold ink, it holds letters—every letter of the alphabet.

Use the letters to complete the words on the next page. (There are clues to help.) After you use a letter, cross it out on the inkwell because you can use each letter only once.

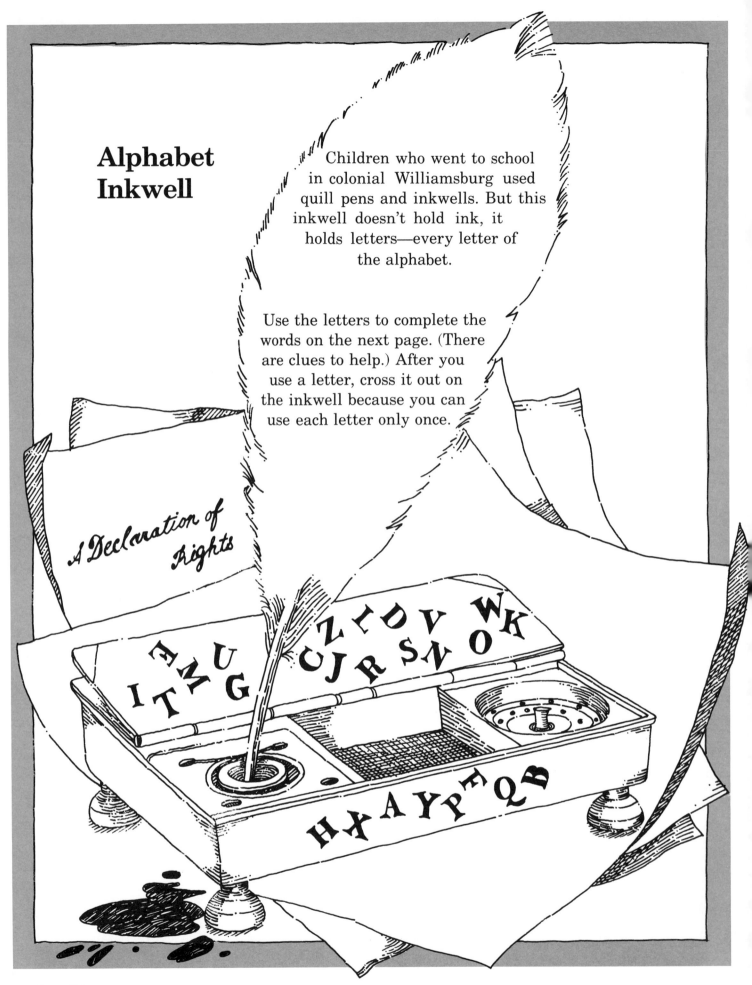

A Declaration of Rights

1. P A _ E R (Goes with ink)
2. _ O O K (Read it)
3. T E _ T (Exam)
4. T E A C _ (Instruct)
5. E A S _ (Simple)
6. S _ B T R A C T (Take away)
7. C O V E _ (Book jacket)
8. R E _ D (Look at a book)
9. S C H O _ A R (Student)
10. K N O _ (Understand)
11. _ L A S S (Learning group)
12. S C H O O L _ A S T E R (Teacher)
13. _ U I L L (Feather)
14. M E M O R I _ E (Learn by heart)
15. S T U _ Y (Try to learn)
16. _ E R B (Action word)
17. _ R I E N D S (Classmates)
18. T H _ N K (Have an idea)
19. H I S T _ R Y (Study of the past)
20. _ O U N (Naming word)
21. E _ A M (Test)
22. A D _ E C T I V E (Helping word)
23. _ X P L A I N (Tell about)
24. T A U _ H T (Gave a lesson)
25. D E S _ (Writing place)
26. M A _ H (Arithmetic)

The A-MAZE-ING Way Home

Help the children get home in time for supper by going through this maze of bricks.

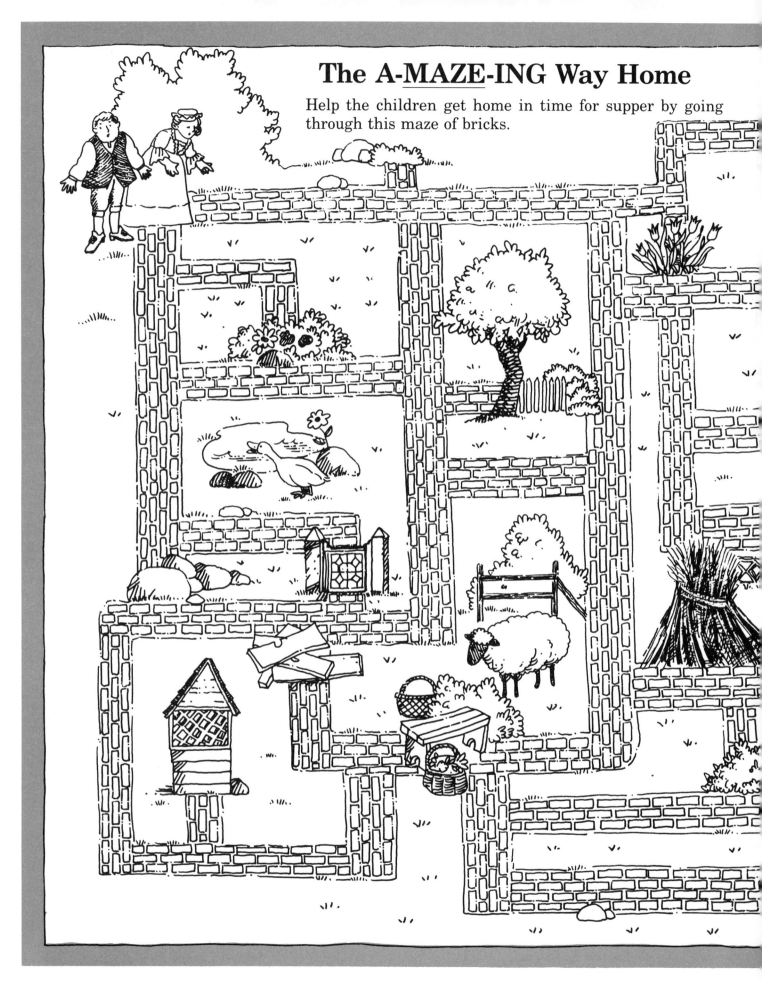

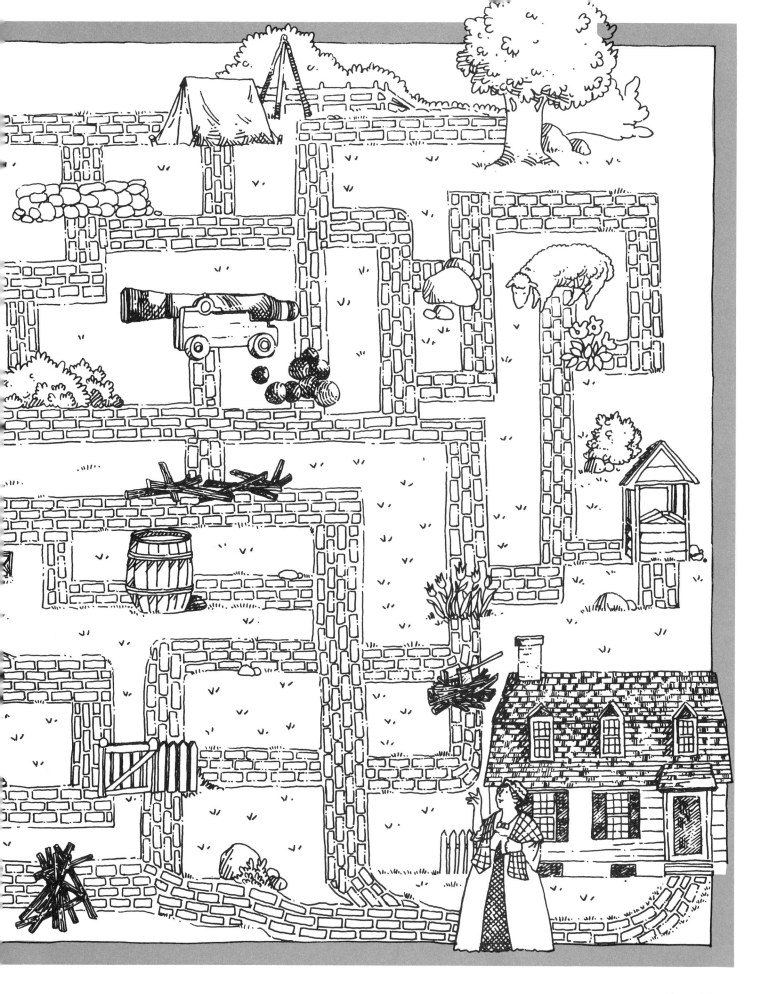

Horse and Wagon
Crossword

ACROSS

1. You and I.
5. One _____ the other.
7. Coaches.
9. Time in history.
10. Go from here to _____.
11. Possess.
12. Opposite of "He."
15. Abbreviation for United States of America.
16. A grown-up colt.
19. Go from here _____ there.
20. Opposite of "Yes."
21. Long, long _____.

DOWN

1. It goes 'round and 'round.
2. When a horse walks quickly, it _____.
3. Travels by horse.
4. Feel the same way.
6. Shape of a wheel.
7. Carriage.
8. Horse _____.
13. Ready, set, _____!
14. Isn't "Isn't."
16. Talley-_____!
17. Word for horse and carriage.
18. Word after "Em."

Special Word List

Everything you need to fill in the squares is right here:

AGO	GO	OWN	THERE
AGREE	HO	RIDES	TO
CARRIAGES	HORSE	RIG	TROTS
COACH	IS	ROUND	U.S.A.
EN	NO	SHE	WE
ERA	OR	SHOES	WHEEL

Hats Off!

All these hats are on—but some of them shouldn't be. **Six** of the hats don't belong to colonial times.

Find them, then take them off by blacking them out with your pencil or crayon.

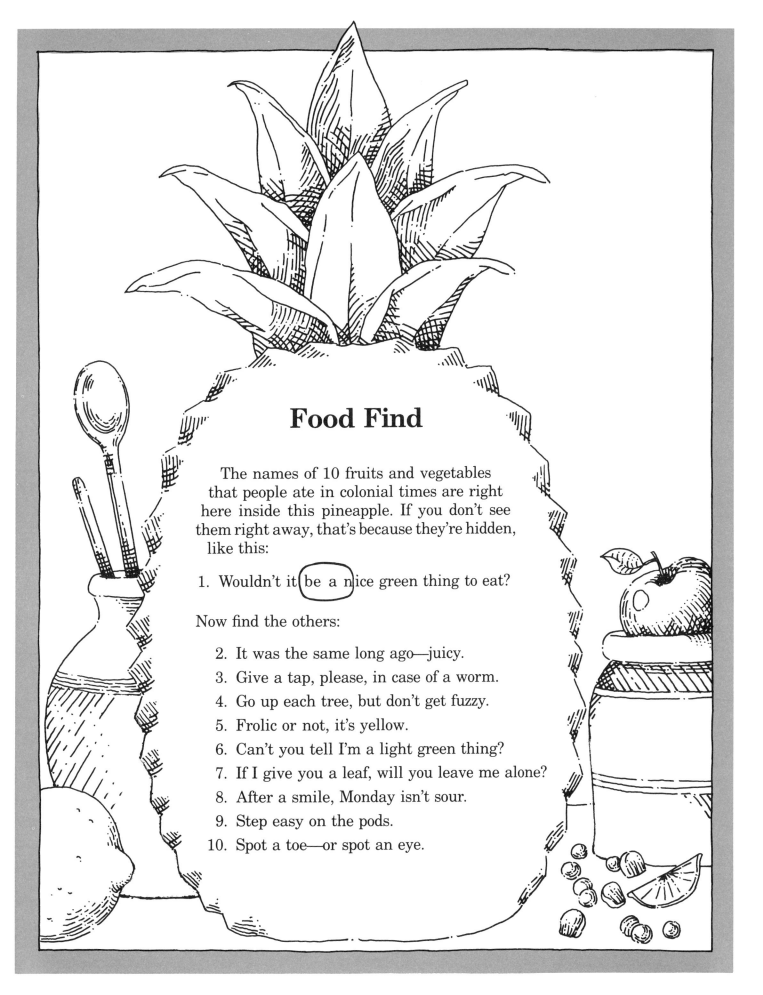

Food Find

The names of 10 fruits and vegetables that people ate in colonial times are right here inside this pineapple. If you don't see them right away, that's because they're hidden, like this:

1. Wouldn't it be a nice green thing to eat?

Now find the others:

2. It was the same long ago—juicy.
3. Give a tap, please, in case of a worm.
4. Go up each tree, but don't get fuzzy.
5. Frolic or not, it's yellow.
6. Can't you tell I'm a light green thing?
7. If I give you a leaf, will you leave me alone?
8. After a smile, Monday isn't sour.
9. Step easy on the pods.
10. Spot a toe—or spot an eye.

Animal Hunt

Hidden in this garden are 10 animals you would have found in colonial Williamsburg. Find them now and circle them.

Music Search

Here are some of the instruments played in colonial Williamsburg. Play around with this puzzle until you find them—by looking up, down, across, and diagonally, backwards and forwards.

BASSOON
BUGLE
CELLO
CLARINET
DRUM
FIFE
FLUTE
GUITAR
HARPSICHORD
HORN
MANDOLIN
OBOE
ORGAN
TRUMPET
VIOLIN

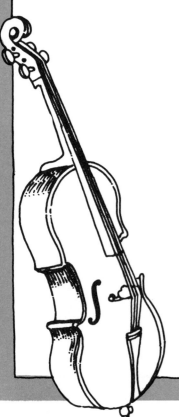

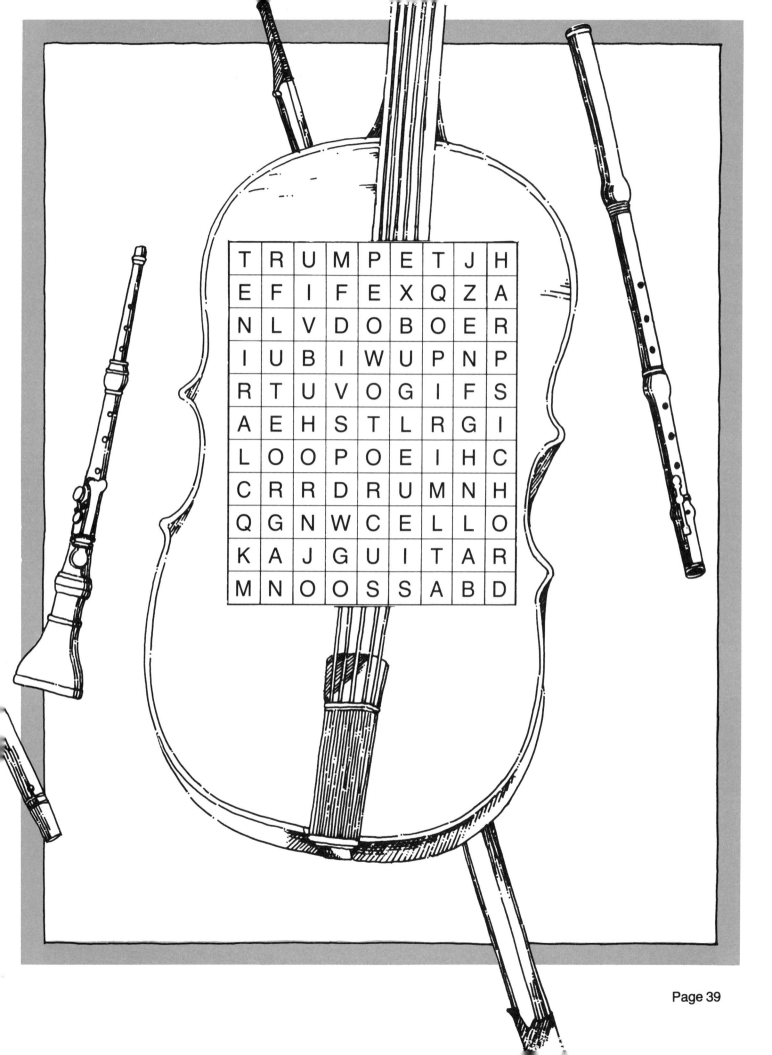

T	R	U	M	P	E	T	J	H
E	F	I	F	E	X	Q	Z	A
N	L	V	D	O	B	O	E	R
I	U	B	I	W	U	P	N	P
R	T	U	V	O	G	I	F	S
A	E	H	S	T	L	R	G	I
L	O	O	P	O	E	I	H	C
C	R	R	D	R	U	M	N	H
Q	G	N	W	C	E	L	L	O
K	A	J	G	U	I	T	A	R
M	N	O	O	S	S	A	B	D

Signs of the Times

As you walk around Williamsburg, you'll see many bright signs hanging above or in front of the shops and taverns. Here are a few of them for you to color. Use their "true" colors, if you know them. If not, use your imagination.

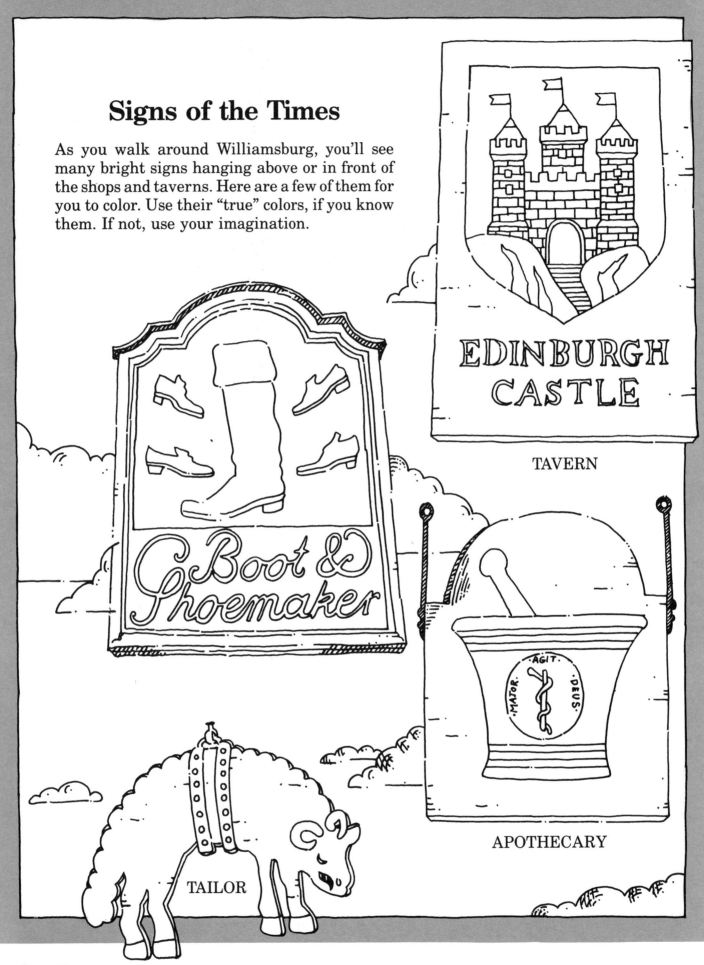

EDINBURGH CASTLE

TAVERN

Boot & Shoemaker

APOTHECARY

TAILOR

Gunsmith

PRINTING OFFICE & POST OFFICE

JOSIAH CHOWNING

TAVERN

M. DUBOIS GROCER

GROCER

WIGMAKER

Barber and Peruke Maker

Which of the Six?

Which of the six soldiers is:

PLAYING A FIFE?
    SOLDIER # _____

FIRING A MUSKET?
    SOLDIER # _____

FLYING THE FLAG?
    SOLDIER # _____

LOADING THE CANNON?
    SOLDIER # _____

DRAWING HIS SWORD?
    SOLDIER # _____

BEATING THE DRUM?
    SOLDIER # _____

Ready, Aim . . . Circle!!!

CIRCLE the soldiers on pages 42 and 43 who are EXACTLY alike.

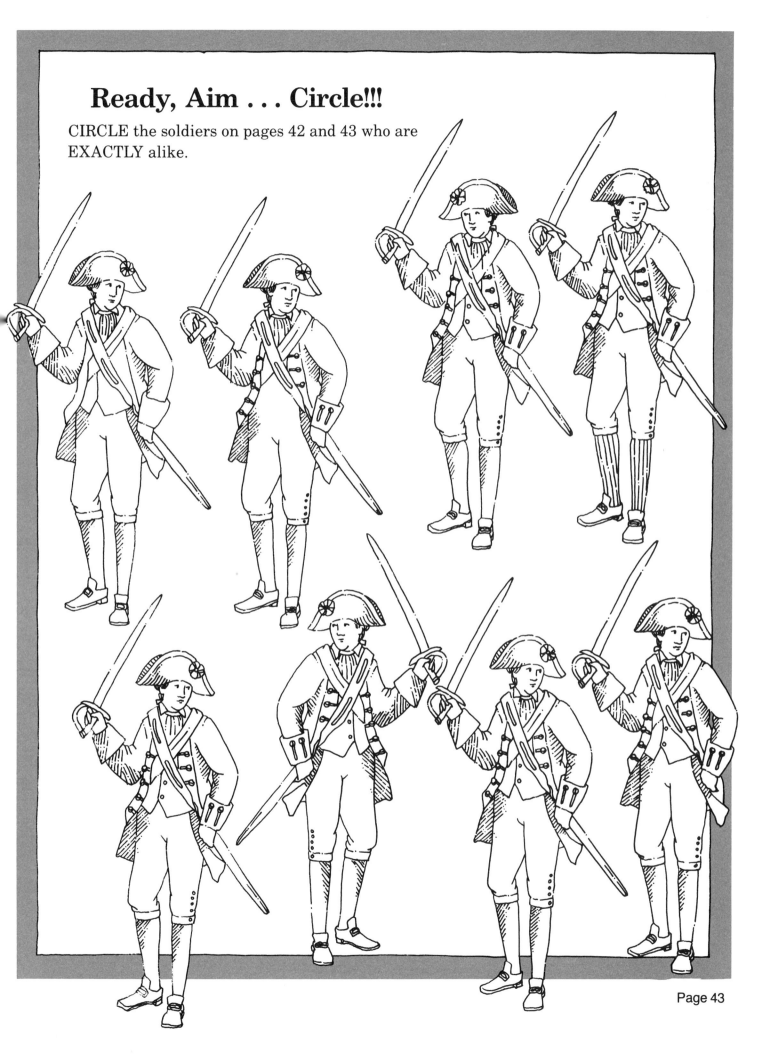

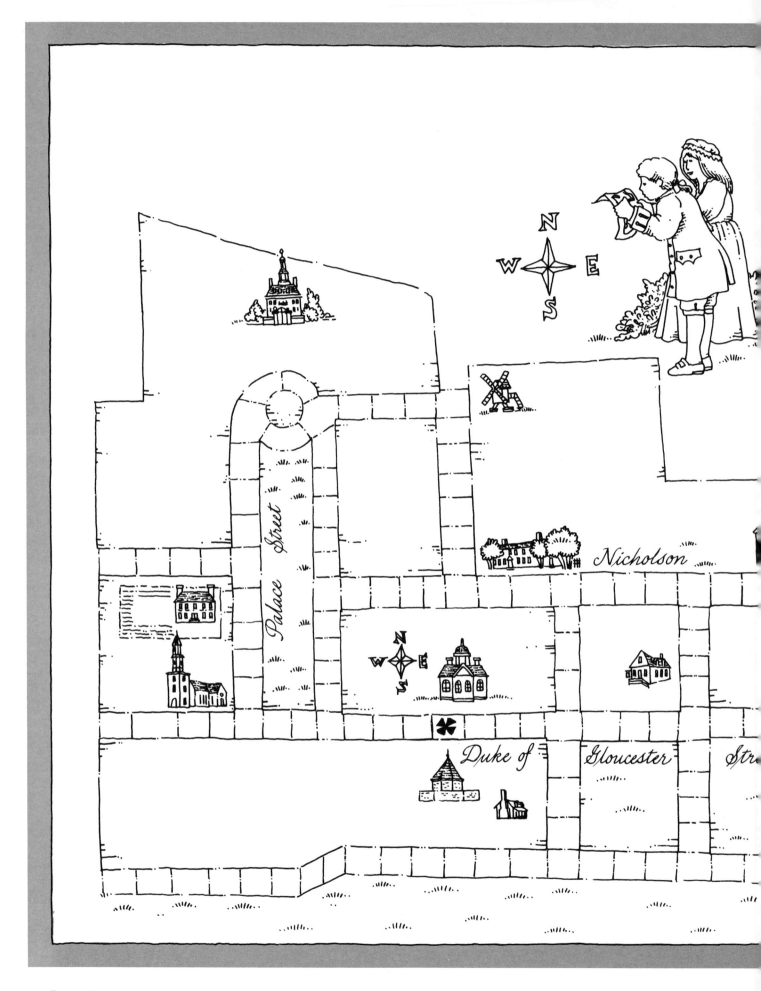

Map A Trip

Pretend you are taking a sightseeing trip through Colonial Williamsburg to see some of the places of interest. Use a pencil or crayon to mark this route:

Begin at the Courthouse on Duke of Gloucester Street. ❈

Go west 7 blocks to the Bruton Parish Church corner.

Go north along Palace Street 4 paces to the George Wythe House.

Visit the Governor's Palace in 6 more paces.

Now go east 6 paces to the Windmill.

Go south 7 paces to the Peyton Randolph House, then walk east along Nicholson Street 9 paces to visit the Cabinetmaker.

Visit the Capitol in 15 paces.

Walk 2 paces west on Duke of Gloucester Street to the Raleigh Tavern, 2 more paces to the Wigmaker, and 8 more paces to shop at Prentis Store.

Go west 6 paces to the Guardhouse and Magazine.

Cross the street to the Courthouse where you began.

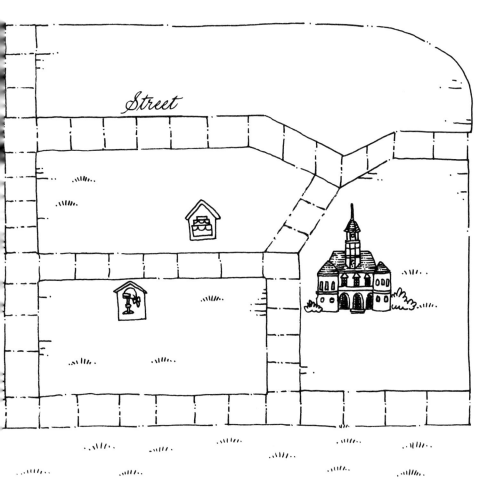

Extra Activity for Mapmarkers!

Find all the places you **really** visited in COLONIAL WILLIAMSBURG. Mark each on the map with a big "X."

The Answers

Page 4 **Tree Search**

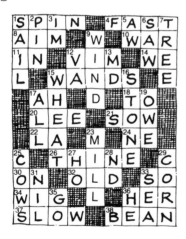

Page 6 **Building Blocks**

BRICK
STONE
PINE
GLASS
PAINT

Page 10 **Windmill Crossword**

S	P	I	N		F	A	S	T
A	I	M		W		W	A	R
I	N		V	I	M		W	E
L		W	A	N	D	S		E
	A	H		D		T	O	
L	E	E		S	O	W		
	L	A		M		N	E	
C		T	H	I	N	E		C
O	N		O	L	D		S	O
W	I	G		L		H	E	R
S	L	O	W		B	E	A	N

Page 12 **Go To Your Room!**

1. YES   7. NO
2. NO   8. YES
3. YES   9. YES
4. YES   10. YES
5. YES   11. NO
6. YES

Page 14-15 **Name the Game**

1. Quoits
2. Fives
3. Stool Ball
4. Shuttlecock
5. Cricket

Page 16 **Picture This**

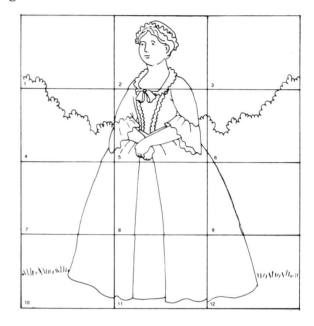

Page 19 **The Gaol Game**

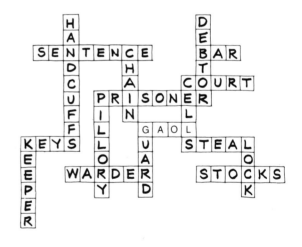

Page 23 **Hurry-Up Gingerbread**

BEAT   STIR
MIX   POUR
SIFT   BAKE
ADD   GOOD

Page 27 Letter Game

SEND
↓
SAND
↓
SAID
↓
SAIL
↓
MAIL

Page 28 Alphabet Inkwell

1. P A <u>P</u> E R
2. <u>B</u> O O K
3. T E <u>S</u> T
4. T E A C <u>H</u>
5. E A S <u>Y</u>
6. S <u>U</u> B T R A C T
7. C O V E <u>R</u>
8. R E <u>A</u> D
9. S C H O <u>L</u> A R
10. K N O <u>W</u>
11. <u>C</u> L A S S
12. S C H O O L <u>M</u> A S T E R
13. <u>Q</u> U I L L
14. M E M O R I Z <u>E</u>
15. S T U <u>D</u> Y
16. <u>V</u> E R B
17. <u>F</u> R I E N D S
18. T H <u>I</u> N K
19. H I S T <u>O</u> R Y
20. <u>N</u> O U N
21. E <u>X</u> A M
22. A D <u>J</u> E C T I V E
23. <u>E</u> X P L A I N
24. T A U <u>G</u> H T
25. D E S <u>K</u>
26. M A T <u>H</u>

Page 32 Horse and Carriage Crossword

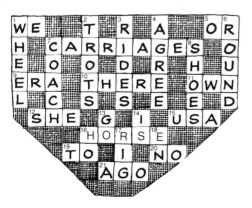

Page 35 Food find

2. It was the same long ago—juicy.
3. Give a tap, please, in case of a worm.
4. Go up each tree, but don't get fuzzy.
5. Frolic or not, it's yellow.
6. Can't you tell I'm a light green thing?
7. If I give you a leaf, will you leave me alone?
8. After a smile, Monday isn't sour.
9. Step easy on the pods.
10. Spot a toe—or spot an eye.

Page 36-37 Animal Hunt

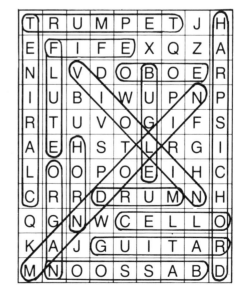

Page 39 Music Search

The Grand Union Flag flies over the Capitol at Williamsburg.

THE END